PENG'S CHINESE TREASURY

Chinese Idioms

VOLUME 2

concept and cartoons
by
Tan Huay Peng

HEIAN

FIRST AMERICAN EDITION – 1987
Second Printing 1991

HEIAN INTERNATIONAL, INC.
P.O. Box 1013
Union City, CA 94587 USA.

First published in Singapore by
Times Books International
Times Centre, 1 New Industrial Road
Singapore 1953

ISBN 0-89346-290-X

Printed in Singapore

CONTENTS

LIST OF IDIOMS

INTRODUCTION

The impact of Chinese idioms

While having a conversation with a friend, scanning the newspapers, following the latest Chinese serials on television, or reading from a Chinese classic — in fact, in almost every situation — we are likely to stumble upon a Chinese idiom.

In the Chinese vocabulary, idioms are significant and integral vehicles of expression. Imagine how often we utter ever so glibly, the following:手忙脚乱, 水落石出, 三心两意, 斤斤计较, 口是心非, or even 一刀两断! Then take an idiom like 马马虎虎, which literally means 'horses and tigers'. To the unenlightened, this would appear totally irrelevant. Where did these horses and tigers materialise from anyway? And to be sure, this is only an example of the many fascinating idioms in existence.

斤斤计较

Proverb or idiom?

As there is much confusion concerning proverbs and idioms, it is best to make a distinction here. A proverb contains a definite message or philosophy of life, whereas an idiom has a wider application. It could either have a moral intent, or be an adept turn of phrase, a cogent expression with no deeper meaning. If an idiom delivers a wise thought or saying, it is in fact a proverb.

守株待兔

一暴十寒

Types of idioms

There are those which are purely descriptive, like 风和日丽 or 古色古香. Some not only describe but seek to clarify and define more concisely. Sometimes they drive a point home by sheer exaggeration and emphasis. 垂涎三尺 and 对牛弹琴 are obvious examples.

A great number of Chinese idioms however allude to something deeper — many carry a moral or maxim, either directly or implicitly. Truly, it can be said that idioms reflect much of the wisdom and philosophy ingrained in Chinese culture.

同流合污

Origins
Although idioms which have arisen from oral tradition and anonymous sources are many, quite a variety have their roots in literary origins, sayings of famous philosophers like Confucius and Mencius, or historical sources. All of these have grown into the heritage which we can richly draw upon.

Idioms and their applications

What accounts for the popularity of idioms? First of all, relatively complex concepts may be fashioned into images everyone can relate to. Instead of declaring that one should not speak irresponsibly and unguardedly, how much simpler to use the visual image created by 信口开河, which clinches the meaning most effectively.

They inject colour and drama to speech and writing, and not just little ingots of wisdom but often much wit and subtle humour, as indeed the cartoons in this book will show. Idioms also have the advantage of economy of thought — the majority belong to the pithy, often rhythmic 4-character variety.

The approach of this book

There are a few thousand idioms being used perpetually in the Chinese language. The 125 explained and illustrated here, cartoon-fashion, are some of the most well-known and oft-heard, and applied easily to most familiar situations confronted in present-day society.

The difficulty of understanding idioms sometimes lies in the inability to see the connection between the literal meaning and its underlying message. To solve this problem, literal translations are highlighted where appropriate, except in cases where the meaning is undisguised, as in 含辛茹苦 or 改过自新. Idioms with literary or historical origins are explained accordingly. There are also sentence examples to show usage.

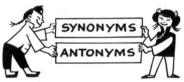

To encourage further reference, synonyms and antonyms, also idioms, are included wherever possible.

The two indexes which form the final section of the book are arranged alphabetically in Hanyu Pinyin and from classification of theme, providing a valuable checkpoint.

津津有味　　jīn jīn yǒu wèi

Literally: Extremely tasty.

Meaning: With relish; with gusto; with keen interest.
Describes one's enjoyment in doing something.

Example: 小琪看故事书看得津津有味，连饭也忘了吃。

进退两难   jìn tuì liǎng nán

Literally: Difficult to advance or to retreat.

Meaning: In a dilemma. The English have an expression:
Between the devil and the deep blue sea.

Example: 他脱离祖国，投奔美国，原以为下半辈子可以过安乐的生活，谁知道在外地谋生困难，落得以洗碗碟为生，进退两难，后悔也来不及了。

Synonyms: 进退维谷　jìn tuì wéi gǔ
Difficult to advance or to retreat.
左右为难　zuǒ yòu wéi nán
Difficulties on the left and the right.

举一反三　　　　　jǔ yī fǎn sān

Literally: To find out three other things from one example.

Meaning: To infer other things from a single fact. This describes one's ability in drawing inferences, indicating therefore comprehension and intelligence.

Origin: The Analects of Confucius. Confucius told his disciples one day: 'If I show a man one corner of a subject, and he is not able to gather the other three from this by inference, I will not bother to teach him again.'

Example: 学生能举一反三，老师也深感安慰。

开门见山   kāi mén jiàn shān

Literally: Open the door and see the mountain.

Meaning: Straightforward and to the point. Can refer to conversation or writing. Not beating about the bush.

Origin: Song dynasty poet Yan Yu (严羽).
'太白发句，谓之开门见山。'

Example: 我们不妨开门见山，坦诚地谈谈彼此的看法。

Antonym: 拐弯抹角   guǎi wān mò jiǎo
Turn bends and go round corners.

慷慨解囊 kāng kǎi jiě náng

Literally: To be generous and open one's purse.

Meaning: Liberal and generous, charitable.

Example: 我国人民纷纷响应报界的呼吁，慷慨解囊，捐助在意外事件中丧生人士的家属。

Antonym: 一毛不拔　yī máo bù bá
Not even wishing to pluck out a single hair.

力不从心　　lì bù cóng xīn

Literally: Not having enough strength to follow what the heart desires.

Meaning: Ability falling short of one's wishes; ability not equal to one's ambitions.

Origin: History of the Han Dynasty.
'超之气力不能从心。'

Example: 我不是不想帮忙，只恨力不从心。

Antonym: 得心应手　　dé xīn yìng shǒu
One's desires are fulfilled.

两全其美　　liǎng quán qí měi

Literally: To satisfy both sides. Perfect in both respects.

Meaning: A situation in which a compromise is met, thus achieving the best of both worlds.

Origin: History of the Jin dynasty. 'To be faithful and filial is to be complete.'

Example: 你把空置的房子出租，可增加收入，而他也有适合的地方居住，这岂不是两全其美？

了如指掌   liǎo rú zhǐ zhǎng

Literally: Understand so completely, as if one were pointing at the palm of one's hand.

Meaning: To have a clear and thorough understanding of something.

Example: 王教授是东南亚史方面的权威，对于马来亚的掌故了如指掌。

Synonym: 一清二楚   yī qīng èr chǔ
Perfectly clear.

流离失所 liú lí shī suǒ

Literally: Wander about without having a permanent home.

Meaning: Become destitute and homeless; be forced by circumstances – like war, floods or famine – to leave home and wander about.

Example: 柬埔寨难民流离失所，境况令人同情。

络绎不绝 luò yì bù jué

Literally: As continuous as unreeled silk.

Meaning: In an endless stream.
To describe heavy traffic or a
continuous and uninterrupted
pedestrian flow.

Example: 此次书展的规模宏大，到来参观的人络
绎不绝。

Synonyms: 车水马龙　chē shuǐ mǎ lóng
An incessant stream of horses and
carriages.
纷至沓来　fēn zhì tà lái
Coming in continuous crowds.

满载而归　mǎn zài ér guī

Literally: To return home well-laden.

Meaning: To have prospered in one's endeavours; bountifully rewarded.

Example: 碰到鱼汛，渔夫们出海必有收获，满载而归。

Antonym: 一无所获　yī wú suǒ huò
To have obtained nothing.

每况愈下　měi kuàng yù xià

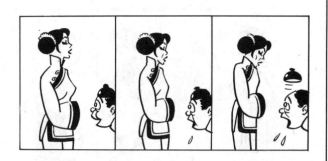

Literally: To decline further with each instance.

Meaning: Deteriorate; get from bad to worse. A steady decline.

Origin: The Book of Zhuang Zi.
'每下愈况。'

Example: 公司的业务每况愈下，得改变营业方针才行。

Synonym: 江河日下　jiāng hé rì xià
The rivers flow downwards daily – things are deteriotating.

Antonym: 蒸蒸日上　zhēng zhēng rì shàng
A steady progress.

美中不足　　měi zhōng bù zú

Literally: An imperfection in the midst of beauty.

Meaning: Not totally perfect. An inadequacy exists which spoils an otherwise perfect object or person.
A fly in the ointment.

Example: 大家齐集一堂，高高兴兴地吃团圆饭，美中不足的是少了哥哥一人。

Antonyms: 十全十美　shí quán shí měi
Perfect in every respect.
尽善尽美　jìn shàn jìn měi
Perfectly good and beautiful.

面目全非　　miàn mù quán fēi

Literally: Completely changed in appearance.

Meaning: Applies to a situation which has changed beyond recognition. Usually, the change referred to here is not a favourable one.

Example: 大火过后，工厂被烧得面目全非，损失惨重。

明目张胆　míng mù zhāng dǎn

Literally: Keep the eyes wide open and expose the gall.

Meaning: Carry on (a bad deed) openly and brazenly, without even the batting of an eyelid.

Origin: From the Tang dynasty.
'丈夫当敢言地，须要明目张胆，以报天子，焉能碌碌保妻子耶。'

Example: 有许多青年男女受到欧风美雨的影响，竟明目张胆，在公众场所搂搂抱抱。

Antonym: 暗中行事　àn zhōng xíng shì
Carry on (usually a bad deed) in the darkness.

明知故犯　　　míng zhī gù fàn

Literally:　Being aware (of one's wrongdoing), yet going ahead to do it.

Meaning:　An act of defiance. Deliberately violating a law, commit a crime, or simply doing what one should not.

Example:　身为警察却受贪污受贿，明知故犯，罪加一等。

莫名其妙   mò míng qí miào

Literally: Nobody can explain the wonder and mystery of it all.

Meaning: A common idiom in daily life, used whenever one comes across something strange and difficult to make head or tail of. Describes unusual behaviour.

Example: 无缘无故地挨了朋友一顿骂，真叫我莫名其妙。

默默无闻   mò mò wú wén

ALL MY OWN WORK

Literally: Silent and not heard.

Meaning: Not well-known, not known to the public. This is an idiom which can be used to describe struggling artists and writers whose works have not attained public recognition or exposure.

Example: 他不求名利，只愿做个默默无闻，辛勤耕耘的园丁。

Antonym: 举世闻名   jǔ shì wén míng
To be known to the whole world.

墨守成规 mò shǒu chéng guī

Meaning: Stick to convention. Do things in the conservative way.

Origin: Warring States period. Mo Zi was a famous peace-loving Chinese philosopher, who was adept in defence tactics, and who, to prevent King Chujing from attacking Song state, successfully defended a city nine times.

Example: 咖啡店的生意冷淡，皆因店东墨守成规，不求改进的缘故。

Synonym: 陈陈相因　chén chén xiāng yīn
Persist in the old ways without any change or improvement.

目瞪口呆   mù dèng kǒu dāi

Literally: Gazing unblinkingly and not uttering a single word.

Meaning: Completely stupefied or overcome with fear, horror, amazement. Dumbfounded.

Example: 空中飞人的惊险表演，看得每一个观众目瞪口呆。

Synonym: 呆若木鸡   dāi ruò mù jī
Stupefied as a wooden cock.

Antonym: 神色自若   shén sè zì ruò
Perfectly calm and collected.

目空一切　　mù kōng yī qiè

Literally: Regard everything before one's eyes as of no importance.

Meaning: An extremely arrogant attitude.

Example: 张雄自恃球艺高超，目空一切，看不起队友。

Synonyms: 妄自尊大　wàng zì zūn dà
Arrogant and self-opinionated.
不可一世　bù kě yī shì
Regard oneself as being superior above all.

Antonym: 妄自菲薄　wàng zì fěi bó
To look down upon oneself, belittle oneself.

弄巧成拙 nòng qiǎo chéng zhuō

Literally: Trying to show off how very clever one is, only making known, instead, one's stupidity.

Meaning: Hidden moral here. A warning to all those who try to outsmart others but end up the fools. One's grand intentions get backfired.

Origin: From Song dynasty poet Huang Tingjian. '弄巧成拙，为蛇添足。'

Example: 想不到我弄巧成拙，媒人当不成，反被两方责骂。

破釜沉舟　　pò fǔ chén zhōu

Literally: Break the cauldrons and sink the boats.

Meaning: Great determination.

Origin: The Historical Records.
This happened at the end of the Qin dynasty, a time of revolt. After his army crossed the river, Xiang Yu ordered the soldiers to break the cauldrons, sink the boats, burn the houses and each take three days' rations so as to show them his determination to win and to urge them to put up a desperate fight. Eventually the powerful Qin army was destroyed and Xiang Yu became a great leader.

Example: 只要我们抱着破釜沉舟的决心，必能战胜困难。

杞人忧天   qǐ rén yōu tiān

Literally: Like the man of Qi who was infernally afraid that the sky might fall.

Meaning: Harbouring excessive irrational fears and anxieties – in fact, so groundless as to be almost ridiculous.

Origin: Based on the fable of the man of Qi, who, being haunted by the fear of the sky falling on him, was so consumed with worry that he could neither eat nor sleep.

Example: 国家虽处在经济不景气中，但绝不会走上天亡的道路，你不必杞人忧天。

Synonym: 杯弓蛇影   bēi gōng shé yǐng
Mistaking the shadow of a bow in a cup for a snake.

千钧一发　　qiān jūn yī fà

Literally: A hundredweight (thirty thousand catties) suspended from a single strand of hair.

Meaning: A very precarious and dangerous situation; to stress that conditions are especially critical.

Origin: Han Yu, an eminent essayist from the Tang dynasty.
'其危如一发引千钧。'

Example: 眼看房子就要倒塌了，消防员在这千钧一发的时刻，救出了困在大窟中的小女孩。

千载难逢 　qiān zǎi nán féng

Literally: Difficult to encounter once even in a thousand years.

Meaning: A very rare opportunity. Once in a blue moon.

Example: 哈雷彗星过境可是千载难逢的奇观，吸引了无数人观赏。

Synonym: 千载一时　qiān zǎi yī shí
Once in a thousand years.

强词夺理　qiǎng cí duó lǐ

Literally: Force explanations and wrest justice.

Meaning: Unreasonable. To insist that something is just and reasonable though it is not.

Example: 为辩论而辩论，有时免不了强词夺理，说些违心之论。

Synonym: 蛮不讲理　mán bù jiǎng lǐ
Unreasonable.

Antonyms: 据理力争　jù lǐ lì zhēng
Argue with good reasons.
理直气壮　lǐ zhí qì zhuàng
With justice on one's side, one is bold and assured.

青出于蓝　　qīng chū yú lán

Literally: Blue is extracted from the indigo.

Meaning: The pupil surpasses his teacher. Or, the next generation will do even better than the previous generation.

Origin: 荀子。'青取之於蓝而青於蓝。'

Example: 儿子青出于蓝，所画的画比父亲的更为传神。

倾家荡产　qīng jiā dàng chǎn

Literally: To lose the family fortune.

Meaning: Ruin and devastation. Used to describe people affected by calamity or disaster. Or to lose one's fortune from gambling it all away.

Example: 赌博不知害得多少人倾家荡产，但可悲的是后来者却不懂得以这作为借鉴。

惹是生非   rě shì shēng fēi

Literally: Provoke a dispute. Stir up trouble (usually unnecessary).

Meaning: To describe people who can't let well enough alone.

Example: 霸权主义国家专门惹事生非，在世界各地制造事端。

Synonym: 无事生非　wú shì shēng fēi
Create unnecessary trouble.

Antonym: 息事宁人　xī shì níng rén
Settle the matter and pacify the people concerned.

人浮于事 rén fú yú shì

Literally: Too many people but not enough work.

Meaning: Too many people are left idle because work is not available for everybody.

Example: 在这人浮于事的社会里，找一份工作谈何容易！

Synonym: 僧多粥少 sēng duō zhōu shǎo
Monks are many but the porridge is little.

人云亦云   rén yún yì yún

Literally: Follow exactly what others have to say.

Meaning: No opinions of one's own.

Example: 我们做人得有主张，不能人云亦云，一味盲从。

Synonyms: 随声附和   suí shēng fù hè
Follow what others say.
吠形吠声   fèi xíng fèi shēng
Echo blindly what is said by another.

任劳任怨 rèn láo rèn yuàn

Literally: Withstand hard work and bear resentment.

Meaning: Stoic; facing life unflinchingly.

Example: 虽然一家大小的杂条都落在母亲身上，但她任劳任怨，从不叹苦。

Antonyms: 尸位素餐　shī wèi sù cān
Not doing any work yet taking the pay.
叫苦连天　jiào kǔ lián tiān
Complain constantly.

日新月异　　 rì xīn yuè yì

Literally: To have changes every day and every month.

Meaning: Rapid progress and improvement, new developments. This idiom is particularly useful when describing advances in the fields of science, technology, etc.

Example: 生活在这日新月异的时代，若不充实自己，便会落在时代后头。

Antonyms: 陈陈相因　chén chén xiāng yīn
Continue in the old way.
因循守旧　yīn xún shǒu jiù
Stick to convention.

如火如荼 rú huǒ rú tú

Literally: Like fire and like a white flower which grows from reeds.

Meaning: Very powerful and mighty. Previously, this was used to describe troops massed together in splendid formation.

Origin: Evolved from the description of two opposing armies. One side was dressed in white uniforms, from a distance looking like a field of white flowers; the other all in red looked like a raging fire. Hence the idiomatic expression.

Example: 礼貌运动已如火如荼地在全国各地展开了。

如释重负　　rú shì zhòng fù

Literally: As if one has been relieved of a heavy burden.

Meaning: Describes the feelings of relief after a task has been completed, and responsibilities are over.

Origin: 谷樑传：'昭公出奔，民如释重负。'

Example: 考完了最后一个试卷，我有如释重负的感觉。

如愿以偿 rú yuàn yǐ cháng

Meaning: To fulfil one's wishes. Successfully realise one's ambitions. To have one's wishes granted.

Origin: From a poem by Huang Tingjian.
'政当为公乞如愿。'

Example: 奶奶下个月去中国探亲，她的心愿总算如愿以偿了。

Synonym: 正中下怀　zhèng zhòng xià huái
Fulfil the heart's desires.

Antonym: 大失所望　dà shī suǒ wàng
Have one's hopes dashed.

三思而行 sān sī ér xíng

Literally: Think three times before proceeding.

Meaning: Have something thought through carefully first, and not simply rush into a decision rashly and on impulse.

Origin: A Confucian saying.
'季文子三思而后行，子闻之曰：再思可矣。'

Example: 凡事得三思而行，不可鲁莽行事，以免出错。

Antonym: 轻举妄动　qīng jǔ wàng dòng
Take reckless actions without due consideration.

僧多粥少 sēng duō zhōu shǎo

Literally: There are many monks and little porridge.

Meaning: If there is overall scarcity, this idiom can be applied. Also, in a society where too few jobs are available, thus resulting in unemployment, this idiom will be appropriate.

Example: 非洲旱灾造成千万人饿死，虽然各国伸出援手，赈粮救济，但僧多粥少，饥荒问题尚未解决。

Synonym: 人浮于事　rén fú yú shì
To be overstaffed; have more workers than needed.

舍己为人   shě jǐ wèi rén

Literally: Sacrifice oneself for others.

Meaning: Helping other people without thinking of one's own interests or welfare.

Example: 影片叙述了两位老师舍己为人，为救被急流冲走的学生而丧生的真实故事。

Antonym: 假公济私   jiǎ gōng jì sī
Serve one's private ends.

事半功倍　　shì bàn gōng bèi

Literally: Do half the work but get double the results.

Meaning: Putting in minimal efforts but being rewarded with wonderful results. Highly productive.

Origin: Mencius said, 'Therefore, with half the effort spent by the ancients, one will get double the result.'

Example: 事前做好周详的计划，就能收事半功倍之效。

Antonym: 事倍功半　shì bèi gōng bàn
Get only half the results despite redoubled efforts.

视若无睹 shì ruò wú dǔ

Literally: Seeing, but acting as if one did not see.

Meaning: Turn a blind eye to. Deliberately paying no attention to what one has definitely seen. Unconcern.

Example: 现代人的心灵几乎麻木了，对于许多不平的事可以视若无睹。

手不释卷　　shǒu bù shì juàn

Literally: The hand not releasing a book. Never without a book.

Meaning: Describes extremely studious characters – or the bookworm.

Origin: Romance of the Three Kingdoms.
'光武当兵马之务，手不释卷。'

Example: 他是个标准的书呆子，终日手不释卷，埋头苦读。

守口如瓶　　*shǒu kǒu rú píng*

Literally: Keep the mouth sealed like a bottle.

Meaning: Able to keep a secret; be tight-lipped.

Example: 你有话尽管说，我保证守口如瓶，不会泄漏你的秘密。

Synonym: 三缄其口　*sān jiān qí kǒu*
Close one's mouth three times.

Antonym: 泄漏机密　*xiè lòu jī mī*
Allow the secret to leak out.

守株待兔　　*shǒu zhū dài tù*

Literally: Stay by a tree stump and wait for a rabbit to turn up.

Meaning: Not willing to work hard, yet hoping to be rewarded by a windfall.

Origin: Han Fei Zi. There once lived a farmer in Song state. One day, as he was tilling the field, a rabbit ran past, dashed itself against a tree and died. From that time, the farmer sat by the tree day after day. No rabbit ever turned up again; meanwhile, his field became choked with weeds, and there was no harvest that year.

Example: 枯坐在家里守株待兔，又怎能找到工作呢?

熟能生巧 shú néng shēng qiǎo

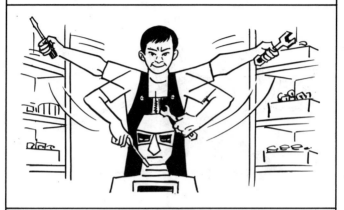

Literally: Skills will be acquired with constant practice and familiarity.

Meaning: Practice makes perfect.

Origin: Records after Returning to the Farm (Northern Song). Chen Yaozi was an excellent archer. During one of his practices, everyone applauded except for an old oil-vendor. Chen was angry. The old man said that his skill was not extraordinary. To show that skills can be acquired with practice, the old man began to pour oil into a gourd through a hole in a copper coin held above it.

Example: 方老伯拉了一辈子二胡，熟能生巧，即使不看谱也能演奏。

束手无策　shù shǒu wú cè

Literally: Have one's hands tied and not know what to do.

Meaning: Feeling of complete helplessness because nothing can possibly be done. A situation which is beyond one's control.

Example: 面对绝症，即使名医也束手无策。

Antonym: 满腹妙计　mǎn fù miào jì
The belly is full of tricks.

水落石出　　shuǐ luò shí chū

Literally:　When the waters subside, the rock will emerge.

Meaning:　The truth will be revealed. Usually used by someone who is determined to get to the bottom of a mystery and states his intention emphatically with this idiom.

Origin:　From an ancient saying of Su Shi. '山高月小，水落石出。'

Example:　只要追查下去，案情总有水落石出的一天。

水泄不通　　shuǐ xiè bù tōng

Literally: Even water cannot leak through.

Meaning: So densely crowded and tightly packed that nothing can get through. Like a barricade.

Example: 球场内挤得水泄不通，想找个座位也难。

Synonym: 比肩继踵　　bǐ jiān jì zhǒng
Shoulder to shoulder – very crowded.

Antonym: 通行无阻　tōng xíng wú zǔ
The roads are clear, obstacle-free.

顺手牵羊 shùn shǒu qiān yáng

Literally: Conveniently lead a sheep away.

Meaning: Seizing an opportunity to take something away. Petty theft can be described in this way. The actions of anyone light-fingered, having kleptomaniac tendencies.

Example: 王大嫂买蔬菜，总爱顺手牵羊，多取一两条葱。

Synonym: 不问自取　bù wèn zì qǔ
Procure something without asking.

司空见惯 sī kōng jiàn guàn

Meaning: A common sight; nothing unusual.

Origin: From a poem by Liu Yuxi of the Tang dynasty. Liu was a Cishi (district magistrate of Hezhou). At a feast hosted by Sikong (minister of public works) Li Shen, they were entertained by a singer. Liu was captivated and wrote this poem: In Sikong's eyes this is but a common thing, but alas! she's broken Cishi's heartstring.

Example: 画家用自己的眼睛去看别人看过的东西, 在别人司空见惯的东西上, 能发现出美来。

Antonym: 绝无仅有 jué wú jǐn yǒu
(An opportunity) occurring only once.

似是而非

Literally: To be wrong although appearing to be right.

Meaning: This idiom is normally used in the context of a warning – that it is not wise to rely or trust in appearances alone.

Origin: History of the Later Han dynasty. '夫俗吏矫饰外貌，似是而非。'

Example: 你说的话似是而非，但我又不知道怎么反驳。

滔滔不绝　　tāo tāo bù jué

Literally: In an unceasing torrent.

Meaning: Any person who is very talkative, hence never at a loss for words, can be described with this idiom. As people who talk too much can be most annoying, the idiom is sometimes used not to compliment but to criticise!

Example: 有的人说起话来滔滔不绝，根本不容许别人插嘴。

Synonym: 喋喋不休　dié dié bù xiū
Chatter tirelessly.

啼笑皆非

tí xiào jiē fēi

Literally: Not knowing whether to laugh or to cry.

Meaning: Certain situations produce a mixed reaction. For example, anger and mirth; or feeling sad and seeing the funny side. This may be so because of a ridiculous element.

Example: 小妹妹把妈妈的化妆品涂了一脸，红一块蓝一块的，叫人啼笑皆非。

提心吊胆 tí xīn diào dǎn

Literally: To lift the heart and hang the gall bladder.

Meaning: Fearful and anxious, edgy and nervous. Not knowing what to expect, one good example being when one is waiting with anticipation for examination results, and if one is expecting the worst!

Example: 当老师喊到小华的名字时，他提心吊胆地走上前，接过成绩册。

挑拨离间 tiǎo bō lí jiàn

Literally: Create discord or a rift.

Meaning: Describes the disruptive actions of a mischief-maker, who stirs up trouble between friends or parties otherwise on good terms, and eventually drives them apart.

Example: 同事之中，就是小丁喜欢挑拨离间，弄到大家不和。

Synonym: 搬弄是非　bān nòng shì fēi
To make mischief.

铤而走险　　tǐng ér zǒu xiǎn

Literally: To run with great haste and meet with danger.

Meaning: Best describes a situation when one has no place to turn and is driven out of desperation to choose the most dangerous path of action.

Origin: Zuo Zhuan (左传).
'When a deer was driven to its death, what choice does it have left?'

Example: 小偷不尽是坏人，也有为环境所迫，铤而走险的。

同归于尽 tóng guī yú jìn

Literally: Be destroyed together. End in common ruin.

Meaning: Usually only in circumstances where, in a move to destroy the enemy, one has to perish as well.

Example: 那个狂人挥舞着菜刀上门，要与变了心的女友同归于尽。

同流合污　　tóng liú hé wū

Literally: To flow with dirty, stagnant water.

Meaning: Associate, keep company with unsavoury characters.

Origin: A saying of Mencius.
'同乎流俗，合乎污世。'

Example: 凡是不愿和他们同流合污，贪财受贿的人，都受到他们排斥。

Antonym: 洁身自好　jié shēn zì hào
Preserve one's purity, refusing to be influenced by others.

投机取巧 tóu jī qǔ qiǎo

Literally: Seize an opportunity and make use of crafty means.

Meaning: Said of opportunists and profiteering folk – who are unscrupulous enough to utilise anything for their evil ends.

Example: 他是个投机取巧的人，连结婚摆喜筵也要从中取利，以劣菜招待亲友，换取大红封包。

头头是道　　　tóu tóu shì dào

Literally: To be reasonable in every respect.

Meaning: This refers to the fact that one speaks with logic, sound reasoning, and that affairs are managed in an orderly manner.

Example: 她虽然受的教育不高，但分析起道理来也能说得头头是道。

Antonym: 杂乱无章　zá luàn wú zhāng
Completely in a muddle; disorganised and disorderly.

徒劳无功　　tú láo wú gōng

Literally: To labour but not produce any results.

Meaning: Spend time and effort, yet have it all wasted because it does not amount to anything.

Example: 我一连试了几次，都徒劳无功，打不开那密封的盒子。

Antonym: 不劳而获　bù láo ér huò
Obtain something without having to put in any work.

望尘莫及　　wàng chén mò jí

Literally: Left so far behind that one can only see the dust raised by the rider ahead.

Meaning: Lagging behind in competence, skill, intelligence. Cannot match up to the other in any way.

Example: 我的棋艺和你相比，真是望尘莫及，只有拱手认输的份。

Synonym: 遥遥领先　yáo yáo lǐng xiān
To be in the lead.

Antonym: 瞠乎其后　chēng hū qí hòu
Lag far behind.

忘恩负义　　　wàng ēn fù yì

Literally: Forget about the kindness and favours shown to us and instead be ungrateful.

Meaning: Bite the hand that feeds you. An ingrate who disregards the acts of kindness shown to him in the past.

Example: 他没想到由自己一手引进公司的朋友，竟会忘恩负义，发表对他不利的言论。

Synonym: 以怨报德　　yǐ yuàn bào dé
To repay kindness with injustice.

唯利是图

wéi lì shì tú

Literally: Interested only in seeking profit.

Meaning: Singleminded about making money, and not bothering about anything else. A primary motive. This is of course an extremely mercenary attitude.

Example: 身为医生，若一味唯利是图，不悉心治疗病人，病人也就不会上门求医了。

Synonym: 见利忘义　jiàn lì wàng yì
Forget about morals at the sight of profits.

未雨绸缪　wèi yǔ chóu móu

Literally: Thatch the roof with mulberry root before it starts to rain.

Meaning: Be well-equipped, make provisions for the future.

Origin: The Book of Odes. 'Turn the soil in your mulberry plantation and bound closely round the door and window of your house before the raining season sets in.'

Example: 如果不未雨绸缪，全面建设起国防力量，将来外敌入侵，就难以保证国家的安全。

Antonym: 临渴掘井　lín kě jué jǐng
Dig a well when one is thirsty.

温故知新 wēn gù zhī xīn

Literally: Revise what has been studied in the past, in order to acquire new knowledge.

Meaning: From knowledge accumulated from past lessons, new and fresh insight can be gained for present application.

Origin: 中庸。'温故而新知，敦厚以崇礼。'

Example: 要掌握一种语文，除了要不断学习外，还得温故知新。

乌合之众 wū hé zhī zhòng

Literally: Like a gathering of crows.

Meaning: A disorderly crowd of people, a mob, a rabble. This can be used to describe bandits, rebels, or even a useless army.

Origin: History of the Later Han dynasty.

Example: 生事的是乌合之众，因此警方一出动，他们便自动解散了。

无病呻吟　　wú bìng shēn yín

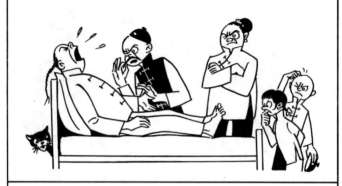

Literally: Not ill and yet moaning and groaning (as if one were actually suffering from the symptoms of the illness).

Meaning: To make a lot of fuss without having actual cause.

Example: 无病呻吟的文章，缺乏真情实感，不能感人。

无动于衷   wú dòng yú zhōng

Literally: Even the heart is unmoved.

Meaning: Showing complete indifference, behaving indifferently even when faced with the most tragic circumstances.

Example: 不管他如何请求，老板都无动于衷，不肯借钱给他。

Synonym: 毫不动容 háo bù dòng róng
Unmoved, unperturbed.

Antonym: 心情激动 xīn qíng jī dòng
Excitable.

无法无天   wú fǎ wú tiān

Literally: Without laws and divine order.

Meaning: The state of lawlessness; acting without any restraint or control.

Example: 反动份子无法无天，竟然置弹炸毁机场。

Antonym: 奉公守法   fèng gōng shǒu fǎ
Law-abiding.

无济于事　wú jì yú shì

Literally: Cannot help to rectify the matter.

Meaning: Indicating that an action is to no avail, because it is too late, or has no effect because it is too insignificant.

Example: 我肚子疼痛，吃了几片止痛药还是无济于事，看来得去看医生才行。

Synonym: 杯水车薪　bēi shuǐ chē xīn
A cup of water to extinguish a pile of burning firewood.

Antonym: 大有作为　dà yǒu zuò wéi
It can be greatly managed.

无所事事　　wú suǒ shì shì

Literally: Nothing to do.

Meaning: Idle away one's time.

Example: 哥哥自毕业后还未找到工作，终日呆在家里，无所事事。

Synonym: 闲暇无事　xián xiá wú shì
Free, nothing to attend to.

Antonym: 忙忙碌碌　máng máng lù lù
Very busy.

无中生有   wú zhōng shēng yǒu

Literally: Create something out of nothing.

Meaning: Pure fabrication, having no basis in reality.

Origin: A saying of Lao Zi.
'天下万物生于有，有生于无。'

Example: 这全是无中生有，捏造出来的，你千万不可相信。

Antonym: 真凭实据   zhēṅ píng shí jù
Conclusive evidence.

五体投地　　　　　wǔ tǐ tóu dì

Literally: The five parts of the body touch the ground – these five parts being the hands, the knees and the head.

Meaning: Kowtowing, an ancient way of veneration and respectful address. This expresses one's utmost admiration and respect for a great deed or achievement.

Example: 我对陈教授的学问佩服得五体投地，希望能得到他的亲自教导。

先睹为快   xiān dǔ wéi kuài

Literally: Derive pleasure from being the first to see something.

Meaning: This describes the eagerness with which one wishes to see or read something new, like a book or a movie. It can, for example, apply to the demand for a new product on the market.

Example: 这本小说一出版，大家就争着抢购，先睹为快。

逍遥法外　　xiāo yáo fǎ wài

Literally: Free from the clutches of the law.

Meaning: Used particularly for people who have committed crimes or offences and yet go scot-free.

Example: 由于缺乏证据，疑凶至今仍逍遥法外。

Antonym: 天网恢恢　tiān wǎng huī huī
Heaven's net stretches everywhere.

小题大作   xiǎo tí dà zuò

Literally: To write a long composition on a trivial topic.

Meaning: Making a mountain out of a molehill, or to make an issue out of something which is really most petty.

Example: 只因为对方说错一句话，就怒气冲冲责问对方，未免过于小题大作。

Antonym: 大题小作   dà tí xiǎo zuò
To do very little about a great problem.

小心翼翼   xiǎo xīn yì yì

Literally: With extreme care.

Meaning: Being cautious and scrupulous in everything one does.

Origin: The Book of Odes.
'维此文王，小心翼翼。'

Example: 我们小心翼翼，一个牵一个，终于平安地走过了独木桥。

Synonym: 谨小慎微   jǐn xiǎo shèn wēi
Cautious and meticulous.

Antonym: 粗心大意   cū xīn dà yì
Careless.

心安理得　　xīn ān lǐ dé

Literally: The heart is at peace and reason is obtained.

Meaning: When the conscience is very clear, and one feels justified that one is doing the right thing, this idiom is applied. In other words, one's conscience is absolutely clear if one can stand firm on one's actions.

Origin: Confucian Analects.
'则心安而德全矣。'

Example: 做完份内的工作，老李便心安理得地取过报纸来翻阅。

心不在焉 xīn bù zài yān

Literally: The heart is not in its proper place.

Meaning: Said of a wandering mind. This commonly used idiom in daily conversation applies to a person who is not concentrating on the matter before him.

Origin: The Book of Rites, a Confucian classic compiled in the Western Han dynasty (206 B.C. – A.D. 24).

'心不在焉，视而不见，听而不闻，食而不知其味。'

Example: 王太太说了半天话，王先生却心不在焉的，一点也没听进去。

Antonym: 全神贯注　quán shén guàn zhù
Concentrating one's entire energy and attention.

心灰意冷　　xīn huī yì lěng

Literally: The heart is grey and the spirit is cold.

Meaning: Discouraged and disheartened.

Example: 只因为情场失意，他就变得心灰意冷，
对什么都提不起劲。

Also: 心灰意懒　xīn huī yì lǎn

Antonym: 兴高采烈　xìng gāo cǎi liè
Exuberant; in high spirits.

心旷神怡　xīn kuàng shén yí

Literally: The heart is spacious and the spirit is happy.

Meaning: Feeling comfortable and relaxed, a favourable state of mind. This idiom does not apply to all comfortable situations, but in most cases describes a person's state of mind when he is in the midst of nature and therefore feels completely happy and relaxed.

Example: 登高眺望，远近景色尽收眼底，令人心旷神怡。

Antonym: 心烦意乱　xīn fán yì luàn
The heart is troubled and the mind is confused.

欣欣向荣 xīn xīn xiàng róng

Literally: Being of lush luxuriant growth, referring of course to vegetation.

Meaning: In general, this means to thrive or to flourish, and also to prosper.

Example: 春天，给大地披上新装；万物呈现生机，欣欣向荣。

Synonym: 繁荣昌盛 fán róng chāng shèng
Prosperous and thriving (describing a country).

信口雌黄　　xìn kǒu cí huáng

Literally: To be careless with one's remarks. 雌黄 is a colouring, which was used in olden times as corrector liquid to remove mistakes made in writing.

Meaning: Totally irresponsible in speech. To speak unguardedly, without restraint.

Example: 为人尊长，怎能信口雌黄，说些不负责任的话？

Synonym: 信口开河　xìn kǒu kāi hé
To be as careless as if a river were being opened.

Antonym: 不苟言笑　bù gǒu yán xiào
Always discreet in one's remarks.

胸有成竹 xiōng yǒu chéng zhú

Literally: Have an image of bamboo in the mind.

Meaning: To be well-prepared. Already having a well-conceived idea or plan before setting forth to undertake something.

Origin: The Song dynasty painter Wen Yuke specialised in painting bamboo. He planted many bamboos around his house and observed them through the year. So familiar was he with its every feature that his paintings were realistic. His good friend Chao Buzhi wrote this appreciative poem for him: 'When Yuke paints bamboo, there is an image of bamboo in his mind.'

Example: 文章如何开头，展开，结束，我在动笔之前已经胸有成竹，所以写来非常顺手。

栩栩如生　　xǔ xǔ rú shēng

Literally: Life-like; realistic.

Meaning: Used to describe how true to life a piece of artistic work is – whether this be in writing, a painting, or a sculpture.

Example: 洞中的千佛塑像栩栩如生，而且神情各异，绝无相同处。

悬崖勒马   *xuán yá lè mǎ*

Literally: Rein in the horse at the brink of a precipice.

Meaning: To realise that one is in a dangerous position and to pull back at the last minute before it is too late.

Example: 王先生悬崖勒马，回到太太身边，挽救了一个破碎的婚姻。

Synonym: 回头是岸   huí tóu shì àn
Turn around and the shore is behind you.

学以致用　　　xué yǐ zhì yòng

Literally: Learn so as to put into practice.

Meaning: This idiom explains that whatever is learnt is of practical value and can be applied usefully.

Example: 这份工作能让我发挥所长，学以致用，是最理想不过的。

寻根究底

xún gēn jiù dǐ

Literally: Search for the root and get to the bottom.

Meaning: Getting to the root or source of the matter, being most thorough.

Origin: Dream of the Red Chamber.
'似你这样寻根究底，便是刻舟求剑，胶柱鼓瑟了。'

Example: 凭着一股寻根究底的精神，他终于彻底搞通了这个问题。

Synonyms: 穷原竟委　qióng yuán jìng wěi
To pursue the source.
追本穷源　zhuī běn qióng yuán
To get to the source.

循循善诱　xún xún shàn yòu

Literally: To guide systematically.

Meaning: Specially used to describe an excellent teaching method, thereby enabling students to increase their knowledge by leaps and bounds.

Origin: Confucian Analects.
'夫子循循然善诱人。'

Example: 在许老师循循善诱的教导下，同学们的成绩有了长足的进步。

摇摇欲坠　　yáo yáo yù zhuì

Literally: Shaking about as if about to topple over.

Meaning: A situation which is unsteady and precarious can be described in this manner. For example, it applies well to a politician or those in power if they are entering a time of instability, or if a person's job is in jeopardy.

Example: 南非白人政权摇摇欲坠，民主的呼声越来越响亮了。

Antonym: 稳如泰山　　wěn rú tài shān
As stable as Mount Taishan.

一败涂地 yī bài tú dì

Literally: Utterly defeated at once.

Meaning: Used in times of war to describe a crushing military defeat, or in a business collapse.

Origin: The Historical Records.
During an uprising in the Qin dynasty, Liu Bang was implored upon to return to Pei County to lead his people. Being modest, though, he said: 'Should the wrong person be chosen to lead the army, you would be headed for sure defeat. Perhaps you had better choose another candidate.' Liu Bang was nevertheless made the leader.

Example: 爱人离去，事业又一败涂地，面对种种打击，他终于走上自杀的途径。

一见如故 yī jiàn rú gù

Literally: Like old friends from the first meeting.

Meaning: To describe the deep attachment and strong bonds of friendship, even if these are people who have only just met.

Origin: History of the Han dynasty.
'白头如新，倾盖如故。'

Example: 他们一见如故，很快便成为好朋友。

一箭双雕 yī jiàn shuāng diāo

Literally: A pair of hawks with one arrow.

Meaning: Achieving more than one goal despite having put in the same effort.

Origin: The History of the Northern Dynasties. Zhangsun Sheng, a general in Northern Zhou, was an archery expert. While on a mission to Turkey, the Turkish king Shefu saw 2 hawks scrambling for food in the sky, and gave him 2 arrows to shoot them down. The general did so, but using only one arrow!

Example: 捐助慈善机构，既做善事，又能扣免所得税，一箭双雕，何乐不为？

Synonym: 一举两得 yī jǔ liǎng dé
Kill two birds with one stone.

一劳永逸　yī láo yǒng yì

Literally: Toil hard once and be forever at ease.

Meaning: To think of the enjoyment that comes once the hard work is over and hence to get something done once and for all.

Example: 地砖破损不美观，唯有打掉重铺，才是一劳永逸的方法。

一毛不拔　　　　yī máo bù bá

Literally: Not wishing to pluck even one hair.

Meaning: Appropriately describes a selfish, stingy, miserly, Scrooge-like person. An exaggerated description of an absolutely miserly individual.

Origin: A saying of Mencius.
'杨子取为我，拔一毛而利天下，不为也。'

Example: 他吝啬成性，一毛不拔，从来不肯掏腰包请客。

Antonym: 慷慨解囊　kāng kǎi jiě náng
Generous, always opening one's purse.

一鸣惊人　　yī míng jīng rén

Literally: Shock everyone with one shout.

Meaning: An astonishing overnight success.

Origin: The Historical Records. King Weiwang of Qi from the Warring States period had reigned for 3 years but neglected state affairs. One day his subject raised this riddle of a silent bird. The king's reply was: 'Should this bird desire to fly, it would soar into the sky at once; should it desire to sing, it would amaze the world with its first song.' Shortly after, the state of Qi prospered almost overnight under his outstanding and able administration.

Example: 她初次演唱，一鸣惊人，赢得观众热烈的掌声。

一目了然　　yī mù liǎo rán

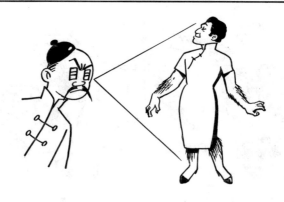

Literally: To understand clearly at one glance.

Meaning: Something so obvious that it is understood instantly. Crystal clear.

Example: 段落中出現主題句，就能使讀者一目了然，明白段落大意。

Synonym: 一望而知　yī wàng ér zhī
To know at one glance.

一暴十寒　　　yī pù shí hán

Literally: To be exposed to the scalding heat for one day and to the freezing cold for ten days.

Meaning: Not persevering in a task, but performing instead erratically in fits and starts.

Origin: A saying of Mencius.
'Even if something had tremendous resistance, and it were exposed to the blazing sun for a day, and to the freezing cold for ten days, how could it possibly keep alive?' The original saying '一日暴之', '十日寒之' was later condensed to '一暴十寒'.

Example: 读书一暴十寒，永远不会有成就。

一视同仁　　yī shì tóng rén

Literally: To regard people with the same kindness.

Meaning: To act without discrimination. To treat all people equally without favour or prejudice.

Origin: Yuan dynasty.

Example: 无论对什么种族的顾客，店员都应抱着一视同仁的态度。

Synonym: 等量齐观　　děng liàng qí guān
Regard equally.

Antonym: 厚此薄彼　　hòu cǐ bó bǐ
To discriminate against one and favour another.

一网打尽   yī wǎng dǎ jìn

Literally: To capture everything in one net.

Meaning: Usually in reference to undesirable elements – the enemy, or criminals seized at once during a police raid. In one fell swoop.

Origin: There were 2 princes of Jin, Yiwu and Zhonger. With the aid of the states of Qin and Qi, Yiwu ascended the throne. However, the ministers had split loyalties. Zhonger's supporters plotted to overthrow Yiwu, but unwittingly fell into a trap; all nine were beheaded. Hence the idiom 'catching all in one net'.

Example: 这帮歹徒无路可逃，终于被警方一网打尽。

一无所得 yī wú suǒ dé

Literally: Nothing is gained.

Meaning: The implication in this idiom is that although effort was put in, for some reason eventually nothing was obtained.

Example: 帮忙别人，本身虽一无所得，精神上的慰藉却是莫大的。

一针见血　yī zhēn jiàn xiě

Literally: To see blood with one needle-prick.

Meaning: Go straight to the point, drive a point home. Those who have sharp tongues would be described in this way when they criticise.

Example: '华而不实' 真是对这篇散文一针见血的评语。

Synonym: 单刀直入　dān dāo zhí rù
Thrusting in a long knife directly.

以卵投石　　yǐ luǎn tóu shí

Literally:　Knocking an egg against a rock.

Meaning:　Fighting a losing battle from the very start because of one's comparative weakness. Heading for certain failure.

Origin:　The Book of Mo Zi (468-376 B.C.). One day, Mo Zi headed north for the state of Qi. On the way, he met a diviner who advised him against going north because his face was dark, and would not be favoured. Mo Zi refused to believe this, saying that his argument was basically weak, exactly like hurling an egg against a rock.

Example:　以一支缺乏训练的军队和训练有素的军队作战，无异于以卵击石，自取灭亡。

以牙还牙 yǐ yá huán yá

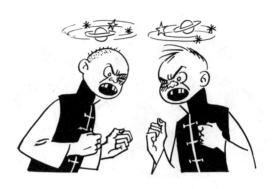

Literally: A tooth for a tooth.

Meaning: Treat other people in the same way as one has been dealt.

Origin: The Old Testament. 'An eye for an eye and a tooth for a tooth' is the complete expression.

Example: 苏东坡作诗取笑苏小妹额头高，苏小妹也以牙还牙，回诗一首笑他脸儿长。

异口同声　yì kǒu tóng shēng

Literally: Different mouths but producing the same sound.

Meaning: In total agreement, unanimously. Everyone holds the same opinion, not differing at all.

Example: 各国都异口同声，谴责霸权主义国家的侵略行为。

Synonym: 众口一词　zhòng kǒu yī cí
All mouths uttering one word.

异想天开　　yì xiǎng tiān kāi

Literally: Imagine that the skies will open.

Meaning: Indulge in wild and ridiculous fancies which have absolutely no grounding in reality.

Example: 科幻小说中的种种神奇想象，当时看来固然是异想天开，但日后也有最终能成为事实的。

Synonym: 想入非非　xiǎng rù fēi fēi
Engage in wild fancies.

Antonym: 实事求是　shí shì qiú shì
Practical and down-to-earth.

易如反掌　　yì rú fǎn zhǎng

Literally: As easy as turning over one's palm.

Meaning: A most graphic way of expressing the ease, the effortlessness with which something is done or managed.

Example: 这件事易如反掌，我包管替你办成。

Antonym: 难如登天　　nán rú dēng tiān
As difficult as reaching the sky.

引人入胜　　yǐn rén rù shèng

Literally: Attracting people into a wonderful place.

Meaning: Describes, firstly, the allure of breathtaking scenery; this idiom also applies to outstanding literary works which captivate the imagination – for example, as in a novel, poetry or short story.

Example: 峇厘岛上的风光明媚，引人入胜。

Synonym: 别有天地　bié yǒu tiān dì
An enchanting place – scenery or works of art.

迎刃而解 　　　　yíng rèn ér jiě

Literally: To come apart when it meets the edge of the knife.

Meaning: A problem can be easily and smoothly solved without involving much effort. Or, an affair can be easily managed.

Origin: The History of the Jin dynasty. 'For instance, a bamboo splits off all the way down as it meets the edge of the knife once its first few joints have been chopped open.'

Example: 只要找到症结所在，问题一定能迎刃而解。

应接不暇　yìng jiē bù xiá

Literally: Too busy to handle.

Meaning: To have too many things to do. Popularly said of a thriving business – more customers than one has time to attend to.

Example: 顾客如潮水般涌来，售货员忙不过来，大有应接不暇之势。

Antonym: 门可罗雀　mén kě luó què
Birds may be caught at the door. A very deserted place.

Synonym: 门庭若市　mén tíng ruò shì
The courtyard is like a market.

优柔寡断 **yōu róu guǎ duàn**

Literally: Weak and lacking in decisions.

Meaning: Best describes those who are irresolute and wavering in character, full of indecision and never coming to a proper decision straight away.

Example: 做事优柔寡断，拿不定主意，就会白白地错过许多好机会。

Synonyms: 犹豫不决　yóu yù bù jué
Doubtful and undecided.
举棋不定　jǔ qí bù dìng
Hold a chess piece and not know which move to make.

Antonym: 大刀阔斧　dà dāo kuò fǔ
Resolute – large knife and broad axe.

游手好闲　yóu shǒu hào xián

Literally: Idle hands and liking leisureliness.

Meaning: Lazy, idling about all the time. A fitting description for someone who is able-bodied but not willing to bother with developing himself, preferring instead to live a life of idleness.

Origin: The History of the Jin dynasty.
'乡无游手，邑不废时。'

Example: 这一伙青年游手好闲，若不引入正途，恐怕会干出坏事来。

有目共睹　　yǒu mù gòng dǔ

Literally: All those who have eyes will be able to see.

Meaning: Obvious to everybody, apparent, plain. Will never go undetected.

Example: 组织散漫，会务不上轨道，这是大家有目共睹的事实。

再接再厉　　　zài jiē zài lì

Literally: Increase efforts.

Meaning: To persevere, strive. Generally used as words of encouragement.

Origin: From a poem by Mengjiao.
'一喷一醒然，再接再励乃。'

Example: 失败了便得振作起来，再接再厉，向着目标前进。

沾沾自喜　zhān zhān zì xǐ

Literally: Smug and complacent, very pleased with oneself.

Meaning: Someone who takes pride in his own achievements, and who is smirking with contentment.

Origin: The Historical Records. Came from a description of Wei Qihou, nephew of Empress Han Xiaowen. Wei was a careless person who thought too highly of his own abilities.

Example: 稍为有点成就便沾沾自喜，那就会使我们停顿不前。

Synonym: 得意洋洋　dé yì yáng yáng
Delighted and smug.

执迷不悟　　　zhí mí bù wù

Literally: To stick stubbornly to the wrong course and refuse to awaken.

Meaning: Unrepentant, obstinately clinging to one's mistaken ways.

Origin: History of the Early Tang dynasty. '惟公执迷。'

Example: 如果你仍执迷不悟，与损友来往，一定没有好结果。

Antonym: 迷途知返　mí tú zhī fǎn
Go astray but know how to return.

趾高气扬　　zhǐ gāo qì yáng

Literally: To raise the toe and put on airs.

Meaning: Strutting about, all puffed up and full of self-importance.

Example: 他升了职，便露出一副趾高气扬的神情，真是小人得志。

Synonym: 盛气凌人　shèng qì líng rén
To put on airs and bully others.

Antonym: 虚怀若谷　xū huái ruò gǔ
A humble mind as open as a valley.

纸上谈兵　zhǐ shàng tán bīng

Literally: To discuss soldiers (strategies) on paper.

Meaning: Vain talk; idle theorizing.

Origin: The Historical Records.
In the Warring States period there was a general called Zhao Kuo in the state of Zhao who was well-read in military science and considered himself unrivalled. But his father Zhao She predicted that it would be none other than Kuo who would ruin the Zhao army. And sure enough, the very first time he went into battle, this brilliant book strategist was killed and his 400,000-strong army was destroyed in one battle.

Example: 刚才我们只是纸上谈兵而已，还得从实践中去求真知。

自投罗网　　zì tóu luó wǎng

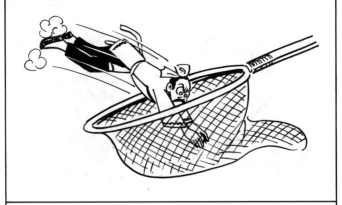

Literally: Hurl oneself into the net (trap).

Meaning: Inflict disaster upon oneself.

Example: 警方接到线报，早已在关口作好布置，只等贩毒份子自投罗网。

Synonyms: 招灾惹祸　zhāo zāi rě huò
Invite calamity.
飞娥投火　fēi é tóu huǒ
Fly into the flame like a moth.

自相矛盾 zì xiāng máo dùn

Literally: Holding both the spear and the shield.

Meaning: Self-contradictory.

Origin: Han Fei Zi. A shield and spear merchant proudly proclaimed that his shield was the strongest in the world. No weapon, however sharp, could pierce it. Then he boasted that his spear was the sharpest in the world and that there was nothing it couldn't pierce through. A passerby asked him: 'What if you try your spear on your own shield?' The merchant was stumped.

Example: 你前言不对后语，自相矛盾，又怎能叫人信服？

Antonym: 言行一致　yán xíng yī zhì
Words are consistent with actions.

坐井观天 zuò jǐng guān tiān

Literally: Sitting in a well and gazing at the sky.

Meaning: Have a limited vision, narrow outlook on life.

Origin: An essay written by Han Yu from the Tang Dynasty.
'Looking at the sky from the bottom of a well, one says, "The sky is small." But as a matter of fact, the sky is not small.'

Example: 知识浅薄却要对不了解的事物妄加批评，这种人正是坐井观天之辈。

Synonym: 井底之蛙　jǐng dǐ zhī wā
A frog at the bottom of the well.

坐享其成　　zuò xiǎng qí chéng

Literally: Sit back and enjoy the fruits of other people's labours.

Meaning: Depending on other resources other than one's own; not wishing to invest any time or effort.

Origin: Mencius.
'千岁之日至，可坐而致也。'

Example: 倘若人人都要坐享其成，不愿吃苦，那国家必然会衰亡。

Synonym: 坐收渔利　zuò shōu yú lì
Profit from others' conflicts.

作威作福　　zuò wēi zuò fú

Literally: Acting like a bully.

Meaning: Tyrannical behaviour, abusing one's power.

Origin: The Book of History.
'Only the king is entitled to exercise the power, to impose punishment or to show leniency.'

Example: 在警方的严厉取缔下，私会党徒作威作福，欺压人民的时代已一去不回。

HANYU PINYIN INDEX

CLASSIFIED INDEX